GREAT
ENGINEERING

BUILDING
TUNNELS

REBECCA STEFOFF

Cavendish
Square

New York

Published in 2016 by Cavendish Square Publishing, LLC
243 5th Avenue, Suite 136, New York, NY 10016

Library of Congress Cataloging-in-Publication Data

Stefoff, Rebecca, 1951- author.
Building tunnels / Rebecca Stefoff.
pages cm. — (Great engineering)
Includes bibliographical references and index.
ISBN 978-1-50260-601-3 (hardcover) ISBN 978-1-50260-600-6 (paperback)
ISBN 978-1-50260-602-0 (ebook)
1. Tunnels—Design and construction—Juvenile literature. 2. Underground construction—Juvenile literature.
3. Civil engineering—Juvenile literature. I. Title.

TA807.S74 2016
624.1'93—dc23

2014049189

Editorial Director: David McNamara
Editor: Andrew Coddington
Copy Editor: Rebecca Rohan
Art Director: Jeffrey Talbot
Designer: Amy Greenan
Senior Production Manager: Jennifer Ryder-Talbot
Production Editor: Renni Johnson
Photo Research: J8 Media

Printed in the United States of America

TABLE OF CONTENTS

CHAPTER
ONE

Going Underground

Two thousand and five hundred years ago, the people who lived on the island of Samos had a problem.

Samos is an island off the coast of Greece, in Europe. The main city was on the coast. Inland, away from the coast, there was a natural spring where water flowed out from underground.

The spring was a good source of water—but a mountain called Mount Kastro stood between the

How can a train travel under a mountain?
By going through a tunnel.

spring and the city. How could the people get the spring's water to their city?

They decided that the answer was to build a **tunnel** through the mountain.

Nature's Tunnels

A tunnel is a passageway that is enclosed, or roofed over. It may run underground or underwater. All tunnels have at least two entrances. You can go in at one end and come out at the **opposite** end.

A lava tube in Volcanoes National Park, Hawaii. After the outside of a lava flow cooled off, the hot inside flowed away.

Tunnels are found in nature. A special kind of cave may be made by hot lava flowing out of a volcano. When the lava cools, it hardens into a long, hollow tunnel called a lava tube.

Many animals build tunnels. Have you ever seen small piles of fresh dirt on a lawn? Creatures that dig tunnels, such as moles or gophers, made the piles. They use the tunnels to store their food, raise their young, and hide from bigger animals that want to eat them.

Rabbits are some of nature's tunnel-builders that live underground.

Rabbits and prairie dogs build huge networks of tunnels called **burrows**. The tunnels connect underground "rooms" and lead to many entrances. Some of the biggest burrows are built by badgers, large members of the weasel family. Badgers have strong arms and long claws for **excavating**, or digging.

Why Dig a Tunnel?

People have been making tunnels for thousands of years.

Tunnels can solve many problems. Prisoners have tunneled to freedom by secretly digging passages. Miners have tunneled into the earth in search of diamonds and gold.

People use tunnels to move things around or even travel without taking up space above ground. One example is subway tunnels. They carry trains and people across large cities, passing beneath buildings and busy streets.

Tunnels have even gone through mountains. When building a road or a railway, it is sometimes easier to go straight through a mountain than to go the long way around! Tunnels can mean shorter trips for cars, trucks, and trains.

Many modern tunnel-building projects are huge and costly. It can take years to complete a major tunnel. But people still make smaller tunnels, too. Small tunnels, called wildlife crossings, pass under streets or highways. These "underpasses" allow frogs, otters, Florida panthers, and other creatures to cross safely while traffic roars by above.

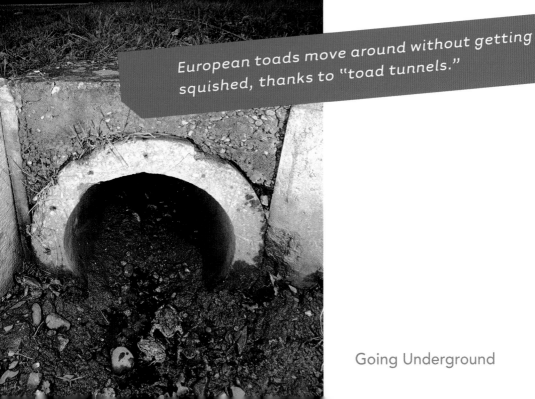

European toads move around without getting squished, thanks to "toad tunnels."

CHAPTER TWO

Planning a Tunnel

Remember the people of Samos, who wanted a tunnel to carry water from a spring to their city? To build the tunnel they hired a man named Eupalinos. He had a special kind of knowledge and skill. Eupalinos was an **engineer**.

Eupalinos the Engineer

Engineers turn ideas into reality. They use science and math to design all kinds of things, from

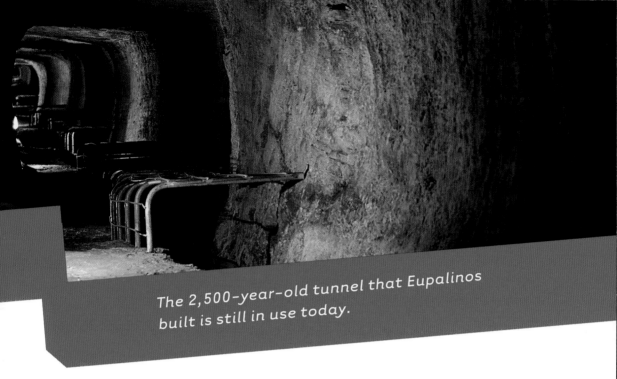

The 2,500-year-old tunnel that Eupalinos built is still in use today.

computers to spaceships. An engineer who designs something big for the public to use, such as a tunnel, is called a **civil engineer**.

An engineer first studies a problem, then figures out how to solve the problem, and finally makes a plan for the work. Sometimes the engineer takes charge of the building process. That's what Eupalinos did on Samos.

He had his workers build an **aqueduct**. This is a channel to carry water over long distances. Most aqueducts bring water to cities from sources far away.

The aqueduct that Eupalinos built on Samos started at the spring. He had workers dig a channel from the spring toward the city. The channel sloped downhill, so that the water flowed through it, but Mount Kastro blocked the way.

To get the aqueduct through the mountain, Eupalinos had to dig a tunnel 3,400 feet (1,036 meters) long. His workers dug into the rock walls from both sides until they met in the middle. The tunnel they made to carry water through Mount Kastro still stands. Visitors to Samos can explore part of it.

Planning a Tunnel

To plan a tunnel, an engineer has to know the answers to many questions.

What will the tunnel be used for? Will cars or trains travel through it? Or both? How much traffic will it get? The answers tell the engineer how big the tunnel has to be.

The engineer also has to study the land where the tunnel will be built. Is it in the countryside or in the middle of a city? Is the ground soft sand or soil, or is it solid rock? Will the tunnel be underwater?

The engineer will probably ask for help from a

geologist, a scientist who studies the earth and what it is made of.

Workers study a blueprint, or plan. It is a detailed guide to building the tunnel.

Geologists can tell how much weight the ground will support, and how slippery the soil is. They know whether there is a danger of earthquakes or cave-ins.

Based on the answers to these questions, the engineer chooses the kind of tunnel to build.

The Three Kinds of Tunnels

There are three main kinds of tunnels: **cut-and-cover**, **bored**, and **immersed tube**.

A cut-and-cover tunnel starts as a trench or channel dug into the ground. It is open to the sky. Once the channel is dug, walls and a roof of **concrete**, metal, or stone are added. Sometimes the surface dirt is placed back on top of the tunnel. This method is used for tunnels that will not be very deep, such as subway tunnels.

Tunnels that must go deep, or through hard rock, are bored tunnels. Boring means driving the tunnel into the rock by digging, drilling, or setting off explosions.

A cut-and-cover tunnel is being built. Later, dirt will cover the top of the tunnel.

Most underwater tunnels today are made with the immersed tube method. ("Immersed" means "sunken.") The sections of the tunnel are built on land. Then they are carried to the water and lowered into place.

An immersed tube tunnel may rest on the bottom of a lake, river, or ocean. Some immersed tube tunnels are buried beneath the bottom. This protects them from **currents**, or movements of the water.

CHAPTER THREE
Start Digging!

Once the engineer has made a plan, work can begin on the tunnel. Early tunnels were dug by hand. Today, building a big tunnel calls for special machines.

The Three Steps in Tunnel-Building

There are three steps to building a tunnel.

Step 1: Excavating

Excavating a tunnel used to be back-breaking work. Laborers would use shovels, pickaxes, drills, or hammers to remove soil or chip away at rock. It could take days for a tunnel to grow just a few feet.

Workers with shovels, carts, and torches build an English tunnel in 1819.

Digging tunnels by hand was dangerous, too. Workers sweated in high heat and breathed the rock dust in the air. Cave-ins were always a risk. Dynamite and other explosives could blast tunnels through rock, but they could also go off without warning.

Today, excavating is a high-tech job. Most tunnels are excavated by machines that are run by engineers and trained operators. Working in tunnels can still be dangerous, but it is less risky than it used to be.

Step 2: Supporting

Have you ever dug a tunnel in sand or dirt? It probably **collapsed** at some point. The ground was too soft or too wet for the walls and roof to stay up.

Builders of big tunnels have the same problem. They used to use wooden posts and boards to keep the roof and walls of a tunnel from collapsing as they worked on it. Today they use a **tunneling shield**.

The first tunneling shield was used in the 1820s to dig under the Thames River in England. The shield was a big wooden box covered with metal plates. Workers inside it dug away at the wet earth. The shield gave them a dry, safe place to work.

Modern tunneling shields are large, curved pieces of steel. Digging takes place under the shield. Powerful motors push the shield forward as the digging moves ahead.

Step 3: Lining

A tunneling shield holds up the roof and walls of a tunnel, but it does not stay there forever. It is only used while the tunnel is being built. As soon as the shield moves forward to a new section of tunnel, workers line the walls and roof behind it.

Tunnels can be lined with steel, concrete, or both. The lining keeps the tunnel from collapsing and also keeps water from leaking into it. Even tunnels excavated through hard, dry rock sometimes need a lining to keep chunks of rock from breaking off and falling into the tunnel.

Special Machines

Tunnel builders use many different machines. Two of the biggest are the **tunnel boring machine** and the **road header**.

An engineer looks tiny inside the tunnel-boring machine called Big Bertha. The yellow tube brings air to the workers. The black belt next to it carries away dirt.

A tunnel boring machine is sometimes called a TBM or a mole. It is a big metal tube that is a digger and a tunneling shield all in one.

The front of the TBM is a flat wheel called the head. It is covered with metal teeth. When the head spins around, the teeth chew through sand, dirt, or rock. The chewed-up earth is carried out of the tunnel behind the TBM.

TBMs are good for building tunnels under cities. They burrow through the earth like moles. The streets and buildings above do not have to be moved for the tunnel to be built.

A road header is like a giant, moving drill or cutter. It crawls forward on a track like a tank. At the front is the cutting head, shaped like a big ball. The head has metal spikes, blades, or teeth all over it. As the road header moves forward, the head cuts or breaks a rock wall into small pieces.

Road headers were invented for use in mines. Today they are also used to build tunnels. People have even used road headers to dig caves for storing wine or living underground.

CHAPTER
FOUR

Under Mountains and Waves

Two of the biggest **engineering** projects of modern times have been to build railway tunnels from one country to another. One tunnel burrows beneath a mountain range. The other dives under the sea.

The World's Longest Railway Tunnel

The Alps are a range of mountains that spread across many countries in Europe. Since ancient times,

A road through the Alps needs many twists and turns because the mountains are so steep. A tunnel could make it easier, faster, and safer to travel.

people have traveled through the mountains at the lowest points, called passes. When people began building roads and railways through the Alps, they dug tunnels under some passes.

The Gotthard Rail Tunnel goes under the Gotthard Pass. It took ten years to build and opened in 1881. The tunnel is more than nine miles long. It carries trains between Italy and Germany.

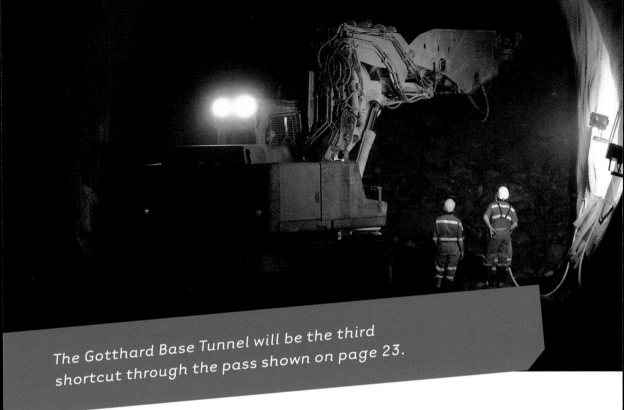

The Gotthard Base Tunnel will be the third shortcut through the pass shown on page 23.

The Gotthard Road Tunnel opened in 1980. It carries cars and trucks beneath the Gotthard Pass. It is 10.5 miles (16.9 kilometers) long. The only two longer road tunnels in the world are in China and Norway.

Now another railway tunnel is being built beneath the Gotthard Pass. It is the Gotthard Base Tunnel. The Gotthard Base Tunnel will be lower and wider than the first railway tunnel. It will also be flatter, so trains will be able to travel through it faster. Passenger trains will go as fast as 155 miles (250 kilometers) per hour through the new tunnel.

When the Gotthard Base Tunnel opens in 2016, it will be more than 35 miles (56 km) long—the longest railway tunnel in the world.

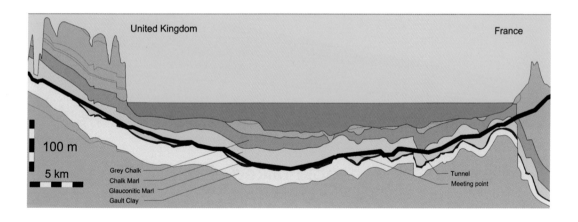

The Chunnel

The countries of England and France are less than 21 miles (34 km) apart, but an arm of the ocean is between them. It is called the English Channel.

As early as 1800, people talked about building a
railway tunnel under the English Channel. In 1988, work
on a tunnel began. The Channel Tunnel (or Chunnel)
between England and France opened in 1994.

Before the Channel Tunnel, travelers could fly
between France and England or take ferryboats

across the English Channel. The high-speed passenger trains through the tunnel are much faster than the ferries. Some of the trains carry passengers' cars and trucks.

No tunnel is perfect. There have been three fires in the Channel Tunnel. Several trains have been stuck when their electricity went out. But the Channel Tunnel has done its job. In 2013, more than twenty million people traveled through it.

The Chunnel has the longest underwater section of any tunnel in the world. Someday, though, an engineer will build an even longer tunnel.

GLOSSARY

aqueduct A long channel, canal, or trough built to carry water from one place to another.

bored A type of tunnel made by boring, or drilling, through the earth.

burrow A network of underground passages and rooms built by animals.

civil engineer An engineer who makes bridges, dams, roads, and other structures for the public to use.

collapse To fall down or break apart.

concrete A blend of sand, gravel, cement, and water that is hard and strong when it dries.

current The flow of water.

cut-and-cover A type of tunnel made by digging a trench and then roofing it over.

engineer Someone who uses science to plan and build things.

excavate To dig.

geologist A scientist who studies geology, the subject of the earth and what it is made of.

immersed tube A tunnel that is built as a tube then placed into a body of water.

opposite Across from, or on the other side of something.

road header A machine with a cutting head that spins around and moves forward on a track, used for excavating tunnels, mines, and artificial caves.

tunnel An enclosed passage that runs through the earth or under the water and has two open ends.

tunnel boring machine A machine with metal teeth on its front for chewing, or boring, its way through the ground.

tunneling shield A piece of equipment that holds up a tunnel's roof and walls, and protects workers, while the tunnel is being built.

FIND OUT MORE

Books

Fine, Jil. *The Chunnel: The Building of a 200-Year-Old Dream*. High Interest Books: Architectural Wonders. Minneapolis, MN: Children's Press, 2008.

Franchino, Vicky. *Tunnel*. Community Connections: How Did They Build That? North Mankato, MN: Cherry Lake Publishing, 2009.

Latham, Donna. *Bridges and Tunnels: Investigate Feats of Engineering*. Build It Yourself. White River Junction, VT: Nomad Press, 2012.

Websites

Building Big: Tunnel Basics

www.pbs.org/wgbh/buildingbig/tunnel/basics.html

How Stuff Works

science.howstuffworks.com/engineering/structural/tunnel.htm

INDEX

Page numbers in **boldface** are illustrations. Entries in **boldface** are glossary terms.

ABOUT THE AUTHOR

Rebecca Stefoff has written books for young readers on many topics in science, technology, and history. She is the author of the six-volume series Is It Science? (Cavendish Square, 2014) and the four-volume series Animal Behavior Revealed (Cavendish Square, 2014). She also wrote *The Telephone*, *The Camera*, *Submarines*, *The Microscope and Telescope*, and *Robots* for Cavendish Square's Great Inventions series. Stefoff lives in Portland, Oregon. You can learn more about Stefoff and her books for young people at www.rebeccastefoff.com.

$28.50

2-16